All of You Must Die
(Spiritually Speaking)

All of You Must Die!

(Spiritually Speaking)

DONALD P. BELZ

XULON PRESS

Xulon Press
2301 Lucien Way #415
Maitland, FL 32751
407.339.4217
www.xulonpress.com

© 2018 by Donald P. Belz

All rights reserved solely by the author. The author guarantees all contents are original and do not infringe upon the legal rights of any other person or work. No part of this book may be reproduced in any form without the permission of the author. The views expressed in this book are not necessarily those of the publisher.

Unless otherwise indicated, cripture quotations taken from the New American Standard Bible (NASB). Copyright © 1960, 1962, 1963, 1968, 1971, 1972, 1973, 1975, 1977, 1995 by The Lockman Foundation. Used by permission. All rights reserved.

Printed in the United States of America.

ISBN-13: 978-1-54565-450-7

DEDICATIONS

This book is dedicated to my Lord Jesus Christ, without whom this book would not be possible. May He be lifted up so He can draw all men to Himself.

Acknowledgments

I would like to thank my wife, Janet Ann Belz, for her unwavering support in the writing and publishing of this book, and my son, Richard A. Belz, for his support and input.

A special thank-you to my mother, Patricia A. Belz, and sister, Connie Evans, for their editing services. Thank you to my family and friends for their support and love in all things.

A thank-you to my parish family at St. Joseph's Church: to the pastor, priests, deacons, and all of my brothers and sisters together building the "City of God" in Ronkonkoma, New York. Thank you all for making St. Joseph's a great place to fellowship and worship the Lord together.

I also need to thank Hope radio, formerly WLIX, and Pastors Rich and Diane Anderson for starting the Christian radio station on Long Island. The music and programming were a very big help in my first years back to the faith and continues to be encouraging every time I tune in to listen. Also from the radio station, I was introduced to the "Let's Talk About Jesus" radio program hosted by Reverend Wayne Monbleau, which was, and continues to be, a place to grow in the grace and knowledge of Jesus Christ.

TABLE OF CONTENTS

Dedications. V
Acknowledgments. VII
Introduction XIII

Newness of Life. 1
Separation 7
The Choice is Yours. 15
Seek and Knock 21
My Treasure is... 27
Spiritual, not Natural. 35
Healing Hearts 41
Who is He? 49
Be Loved. 55
Perfect? 61
Turn Around. 69
Pick Up Your Cross. 75
Last Chapter 81

INTRODUCTION

The purpose of this book, of every chapter and every page, is to encourage my brothers and sisters in Christ to, "grow in the grace and knowledge of our Lord Jesus Christ"(2Peter 3:18) "with a simplicity and purity of devotion to Him"(Paul, 2 Cor. 11:3). I am writing this for the Church, for those who have received Jesus as Lord and Savior, and to all who would call themselves Christians, regardless of the denomination that you may be a part of: we are all the Body of Christ.

To those who barely know Him at all, I tell you His word is always, "Come, learn of me for I am meek and humble of heart"(Matt. 11:29). To those who spend time with Him in prayer and worship, and who are in the Word every day, I tell you His word is always, "Come, learn of me for I am meek and humble of heart" (Matt. 11:29). For everyone in between, His word is the same; for He is the same now and forevermore. He who was, is, and ever shall be, the Father, the Son and the Holy Spirit, one God forever and ever.

It is my hope and prayer that you will be encouraged to deepen your relationship with Jesus. That you will find yourself wanting to spend time with Him in prayer, in worship, and in the Scriptures. I know once you taste and see the goodness of the Lord, it will be your joy to continue walking with Him every day. Get to know Him and you will find that He truly is, "The friend that sticks closer than a brother" (Prov. 18:24). Receive, live, and enjoy the abundant life that Jesus has for you.

May God bless you on your journey.

Newness of Life

All of you must die is more than just a catchy title; it is the truth. All of us have died, all who have been baptized in His name.

> Or are you unaware that we who were baptized into Christ Jesus were baptized into His death? We were indeed buried with Him through baptism into death, so that, just as Christ was raised from the dead by the glory of the Father, we too might live in newness of life.
> (Romans 6:3)

According to Paul, we have already died through our baptism. The journey of our death and new life starts when we accept this truth and begin to grow in the understanding of it.

The last part of this verse in Romans is the one that causes the trouble, "we too might live in newness of life." That word "might" implies that we also "might not" live in newness of life. It looks like there is a choice to be made; and there is always a choice to be made. Each and every day, we have choices to make concerning how we live our lives. God has given us free will so that we will freely choose Him; not just follow laws written on stone but live in "newness of life" with Him. Paul continues in Romans about our death and the newness of life:

> For if we have grown into union with Him through a death like His, we shall also be united with Him in the resurrection. We know that our old self was crucified with Him, so that our sinful body might be done away with, that we might no longer be in slavery to sin. For a dead person has been absolved from sin. If then, we have died with Christ, we believe that we shall also live with Him. We know that Christ, raised from the dead, dies no more; death no longer has power over Him. As to His death, He died to sin once for all; as to His life, He lives for God. Consequently,

> you too must think of yourselves as being dead to sin and living for God in Christ Jesus.
> (Romans 6:5-11)

This is newness of life, being dead to sin and living for God in Christ Jesus.

Who or what could, who or what would, keep us from this "newness of life" that Paul is talking about? The choice is yours; it is always up to you. The first step is always the hardest. The first step is to truly accept and understand that you have died, because all of you must die. Only after death can there be a resurrection, a resurrection to a life in Christ: a life lived in the light, not in darkness; a life lived in His righteousness, not our own; a life of joy and peace and love. Jesus died to give you this kind of life, and it is yours if you would only receive it for yourself. Jesus is holding nothing back: "For however many are the promises of God, their Yes is in Him" (2 Cor. 1:20). As I said in the introduction, Jesus's word to everyone is to, "Come, learn of me for I am meek and humble of heart" (Matt. 11:29).

May we all make the choice daily to live in the "newness of life" with Jesus and grow

ALL OF YOU MUST DIE ! (SPIRITUALLY SPEAKING)

in the grace and knowledge of Him, with a simplicity and purity of devotion to Him.

Separation

If the choice has been made to follow Jesus, we must be prepared for the consequences.

> If the world hates you, realize that it hated me first. If you belonged to the world, the world would love its own; but because you do not belong to the world, and I have chosen you out of this world, the world hates you.
> (John 15:18)

These are the words of Jesus, so you can count on them being true. A life following Jesus will cause a separation from the world, but this is a good thing. The world cannot offer you any of the things that Jesus offers: love, peace, joy, happiness, fulfillment, and, of course, reconciliation with God the Father.

Following Jesus will put you in opposition to many things the world teaches and views as important: look out for number one; do whatever it takes to get ahead; focus on yourself and your wants and needs; basically live for yourself. This is not how a follower of Jesus lives life.

> None of us lives for oneself, and no one dies for oneself. For if we live, we live for the Lord, and if we die we die for the Lord; so that, whether we live or die, we are the Lord's. For this is why Christ died and came to life, that He might be Lord of both the dead and the living.
> (Romans 14:7)

When I think of the world, I am not talking about the people in the world: but the systems of the world, the ideologies of the world, the thoughts and ideas that are put out by the world, as to what life is about and how it should be lived. Many religious people seem to make an enemy of the people in the world: I'm right-and-they're-wrong-kind of thing, and if they don't straighten up they will go straight to hell. I think this is a mistake. We all need to remember, "God so loved the world that He gave His only Son, so that everyone who believes in Him might not perish but might have eternal life" (Jn. 3:16). This is how God sees the people in the world. He loves us. He loves us all. We also must love. We must love everyone.

Jesus said that we should love our enemies and pray for those that persecute us (Matt. 5:44); this is what we are called to do. Many people, believers and non-believers alike, have trouble understanding this scripture. Why would I love someone who doesn't love me? Why would I pray for someone who has done me harm? This is something that will separate us from the world. More important than what was done to us or against us is the truth that we are called to lead people to Jesus Christ. We must show others the love of God in all of our actions, even to our enemies, maybe even especially our enemies, so that they might be led to the Lord. This is not an easy thing to do; in fact, it may not even be possible for us, but it is possible for Jesus. We all must die to whatever gets in the way of us loving someone, so that Jesus can love them through us.

Loving even our enemies, loving everyone, actually frees you from things in life, like bitterness, anger, and cynicism. When you love someone, you see the best in them; you give them the benefit of the doubt in any given situation. You are more likely to try to see things from their side and try to understand why they would do or say something. You become more compassionate and less judgmental toward everyone. The more you do this, the easier it will get, until one day you realize a great truth: there are no enemies. No enemies except one; he is a liar and a thief and comes only to kill and destroy (John 10:10). Once you see that there are no enemies, only people that haven't met Jesus yet, there is nothing to do but feel compassion for them.

This is what having a relationship with Jesus helps us to do. He can turn a heart of stone into a heart of flesh. He can take a hardened heart and make it soft and pliable, if we only let Him. First, our own hearts; then, the hearts of those that are in our lives through us. The benefits to us are endless, and they show up in the quality and joy of our lives. I believe you will find yourself with a smile on your face more often and being genuinely happier in life. There will be a noticeable weight lifted off of your shoulders. How wonderful it is to not have to make a judgment about everyone you see and meet; just to see him/her as one of God's children, a fellow brother and sister in the Lord. Maybe someone who has never met Jesus will now meet Him through you.

What a blessing it is when you show someone the love, grace, and mercy of the Lord and the person receives it for him/herself. This is what evangelization is all about, introducing people to Jesus. It's showing people who Jesus is, and what He has done for us, simply by living our lives with Him and letting Him live through us; in the things we say and do, and sometimes, more importantly, in the things that we don't say and do. Jesus said, "When I am lifted up, I will draw all men to myself" (Jn. 12:32). I just need to lift Him up; He will do the rest. As Peter said, "Always be ready to give an explanation to anyone who asks you for a reason for your hope, but do it with gentleness and reverence, keeping your conscience clear..." (1 Pet. 3:15). Jesus is the reason for my hope. Jesus helps me to see things in a new light, in His light. Jesus helps me to see a bigger picture than my immediate circumstance and helps me through, around, or over whatever situation I find myself in presently. He has proven Himself faithful to me every day of my life; even when I was faithless, He remained faithful. He will be faithful to you also.

My friends, I pray you will make the choice to follow Jesus, not the world. Do not follow after the world and worldly things. Rather, lead the world, lead the world to Jesus. "Draw near to Him and He will draw near to you" (James 4:8). "Walk in the light as He is in the light" (1 Jn. 1:7). May God bless you each and every day, as you walk with your Savior, the Son of God, Jesus the Christ.

Amen.

The Choice is Yours

The choice to follow Jesus should not be taken lightly. If you have been called, if you have received Him as Lord and Savior, that is the most important choice in life you can make. A new disciple of Jesus, or an old disciple that has returned to the faith, now has a line drawn in the sand. There is now a life before Jesus and a new life with Him, in Him. "No one who sets a hand to the plow and looks to what was left behind is fit for the kingdom of God" (Lk. 9:62). There is no room for indecision; there is a yes or no needed, that's all. When I first came back to the faith, and had the revelation that God was real and Jesus is the Son of God, I wanted to learn everything I could about Him. I soon realized how little I knew. Thirty-eight years of going to church, hearing the stories in the Bible, I finally had a kernel of the light of truth and it was awesome!

The mistake I had made for my whole life was that I thought I knew Jesus. I would have told you I thought He was the Son of God, that He paid the price for my sins at the cross. He cured diseases; He raised people from the dead. I believed He was raised from the dead and is seated at the right hand of the Father. All of this and more I could have told you I believed and I did, but I believed it like I believe the North won the Civil War. As I learned about it in history class, I learned about Jesus in religion class. These events happened in the past, because Jesus wasn't real to me in the present. He was not a part of my daily life in any meaningful way. I knew the Golden Rule; I wouldn't purposefully hurt anyone, and I was a "good" person. At the time I wasn't going to church every Sunday. I figured God knows me; He knows I'm not a bad person. I do the best I can. I thought that being good and helping people when I can was what was important. It is, but it is not even close to what having a relationship with Jesus is all about; not even close.

Having a relationship with Jesus, being born again, being saved, being in the newness of life with Jesus Christ, is a life-changer. It is that line drawn in the sand of our lives. It does not, however, make you instantly perfect. It does not mean you will never have questions or doubts or never fall down. It does not mean pain and suffering will not touch you anymore. What it does mean is that you now have someone to turn to in every situation in which you find yourself. You can "cast all your worries upon Him for He cares for you" (1 Pet. 5:7). He is a "very present help in time of trouble" (Ps. 46:1). He will lift you up when you are down. He will rejoice when you rejoice and weep with you when you weep. He truly is a "friend who sticks closer than a brother" (Prov. 18:24). Jesus said, "In this world you will have tribulation, but be of good cheer, for I have overcome the world" (Jn. 16:33). A life in Christ helps you to overcome the world. I have found that Jesus will straighten the crooked path, lift up the valley, lower the mountain, and smooth out the bumpy road.

One of the things, and there are many, that I love about my walk with Jesus is that it is MY walk. It is not yours or anyone else's. Our relationship is one of a kind, because each of us is one of a kind. Jesus loves, teaches, heals, and encourages all of us right where we are. He knows what we need, when we need it, and His supply for all of our needs is limitless.

The one thing I don't like about my walk with Jesus is that I can't give it to you. I cannot give anyone the gift of my relationship with Jesus. I can tell you how awesome it is, and it is. I can tell you how amazing He is, and He is. I cannot give you a close relationship with Him, though I wish I could. Like any relationship, a relationship with Jesus takes time: time spent in prayer, time spent reading and meditating on the Scriptures; time spent in worship; time spent simply being still and knowing that He is God. This is how we grow in the grace and knowledge of our Lord Jesus Christ.

So, my friends, you have made the correct choice to follow Jesus. It's a choice that will yield its fruit thirty-fold, sixty-fold, a hundredfold over the course of your lives and into eternity. Don't look back to what is left behind but look forward to a life of joy, peace, and love in the Holy Spirit. You are truly starting on the journey of a lifetime. Even if you have been with the Lord for years, each day can be like the first because the more you learn, the more you see how little you know. For there is no end to the depth of the riches that are in Christ Jesus. He just gets better and better the more you know and learn of Him.

Seek and Knock

Come to me, all you who labor and are burdened, and I will give you rest. Take my yoke upon you and learn from me, for I am meek and humble of heart; and you will find rest for yourselves. For my yoke is easy, and my burden light.
(Matthew 11:28)

This is one of my favorite scriptures. I wonder if we took a survey how many people would have being meek and humble of heart on their to-do list? How many of us have this as the direction for our lives? All of us that call ourselves Christians should answer with a resounding yes. This is what Jesus says to do, and He tells us the reward is rest for our souls. Sounds good to me. Who would not want some more rest in their lives? I don't know too many people that get enough rest or couldn't use some more.

"Learn from me, for I am meek and humble of heart." This is an invitation for all of us to enter into the newness of life each day with Jesus. Each and every day He invites us to spend time with Him, to learn of Him, to learn from Him. Every day He has new things to show us, new things to teach us, new revelations for those whose hearts and minds are open to receive them. This is an amazing way of life for those who would choose it. It's exciting to be shown new things; to look at a situation with new eyes and have an understanding you never had before. Jesus does not lie; those that seek will find(Matt 7:7). Those that knock, the door will be opened to them. The choice is still ours, the choice is always ours to make; it is on us to seek, it is on us to knock.

The most obvious place to start our search, the first door we should knock on, should be the Word of God, the Holy Scriptures, the Bible. It is in the pages of the Bible that we begin to learn about Jesus: what He is like, His character, His priorities, His purpose, His teachings. "The Son is the radiance of God's glory and the exact representation of his being" (Heb. 1:3). Learning of Jesus teaches us about God. Like Jesus told Philip, "he who has seen me has seen the Father" (Jn. 14:9).

I used to look at the Bible as a book of right and wrong, how to keep on the straight and narrow and be a "good" person. The Bible does cover these things, but there is so much more to it. As I started reading and learning each day, listening to different people preach the Word and really paying attention in our church service, the words of scripture would come into my mind during my everyday life. Now they had meaning to me.
Understanding started to come in applying the scripture to what was happening in life today. It wasn't long until the book of right and wrong became like a treasure map. On this page, joy, over here encouragement, over there wisdom. Turn the page there's knowledge, truth, grace, mercy, and love on every page. Jesus teaches us all in these pages about Himself. He shows us who He is, and we learn who we are in Him. What a wonderful Savior we have; what a wonderful God we serve!

All of us must die to whatever it is that gets in our way of reading the word of truth found in the Bible. Please, my brothers and sisters, open the pages of scripture with an open heart and an open mind. The treasures waiting for you cannot even be counted, for they number as the stars. You will never find a greater return on your investment of time than time spent with Jesus. His rewards are for here and now and into eternity. Open the Scriptures today and begin to "grow in grace and in the knowledge of our Lord and Savior Jesus Christ" (2 Pet. 3:18).

My Treasure is...

"Learn from me, for I am meek and humble of heart" (Matt. 11:29).

The trouble with this scripture is that meekness and humility are not qualities esteemed in the world. How am I supposed to get ahead in the world by being meek and humble? The answer is simple; you're not. The riches Christ speaks of are spiritual, not of this world. We, as Christians, are not called to "get ahead in the world"; we are called to "overcome the world." "In the world you will have trouble, but take courage, I have conquered the world" (Jn. 16:33). In John 17:16, "They do not belong to the world any more than I belong to the world." This gets back again to the separation from the world that comes with following Jesus. The world will tell you he that dies with the most toys wins. Jesus says,

> Do not store up for yourselves treasures on earth, where moth and decay destroy, and thieves break in and steal. But store up treasures in heaven, where neither moth nor decay destroy, nor thieves break in and steal. For where your treasure is, there also will your heart be.
> (Matthew 6:19).

This seems to be a scripture where the rubber meets the road. Where is your treasure? Is your treasure in this world? Or, is your treasure in Christ? Everything in this world is temporary in the light of eternity. If you find joy in this world, it will not last. If you find peace in the world, it will not last. If you find happiness in this world, it will not last! These are things that the world simply cannot offer you for very long. When you acquire something new you have wanted, it soon loses its luster and you look for something else. When you find the peace, joy, and happiness that comes from Jesus Christ, it will never fade; it is eternal. These are qualities of life only Jesus can truly give you: a peace beyond under-standing; a joy that remains with you always, because Jesus remains with you always.

Even in tough times, these words are true. In James, chapter 1 verse 2, "consider it all joy, my brothers, when you encounter various trials, for you know that the testing of your faith produces perseverance." Or in Matthew, chapter 5 verse 11, "blessed are you when they insult you and persecute you and utter every kind of evil against you because of me. Rejoice and be glad, for your reward will be great in heaven."

So I would encourage you to think and pray on this scripture: "where your treasure is, there also will your heart be(Matt 6:19)." I truly believe that if you spend any time with Jesus, you will find that "we have been blessed in Christ with every spiritual blessing in the heavens" (Eph. 1:3). You will taste and see the goodness of the Lord, and the answer of where your true treasure is will become very clear. All you have to do is die. Die to the lure of the riches of this world and allow Christ in you to show you His immea-surable riches. Our treasure, treasures beyond anything this world can offer you, are found in Christ Jesus.

    This reminds me of the parable of the man who found a treasure in a field. What did he do? He sold everything he had and bought that field. This, Jesus says, is what the kingdom of heaven is like. When you know the treasure you have in Christ, you can let go of what counts as treasure in this world. I have found that as you continue in a daily walk with Jesus, this happens with less effort than you would think. It doesn't happen overnight, but Jesus works on your heart in so many ways that without even realizing it maybe, one day, you find your priorities have changed. What was valuable to you in the past doesn't seem worth the time or trouble it used to cause. As you keep walking with Jesus, you will see how many people chase after the treasures of this world and the merry-go-round they are on, never really reaching a place of peace or happiness but forever chasing it. Round and round they go until they realize, hopefully, that the world cannot give them what the world does not have.

    Jesus will take you off of the merry-go-round and onto a path of peace, love, and joy that only He can truly give. "But seek first His kingdom of God and His righteousness, and all these things will be given you besides" (Matt. 6:33). The untold riches of a life in Christ await you, my friends; you need only take His hand. "Learn of me, for I am meek and humble of heart (Matt 11:29)." It is really that simple; take His hand and don't let go.

Spiritual, not Natural

I think what we as the Body of Christ have done is we have naturalized what is a spiritual path. I think we would all agree that Jesus was a spiritual person. It stands to reason then that would-be followers of Jesus, Christians, would be spiritual people too. We are no longer in the natural man, as in Adam, but are part of the spiritual Body of Christ, of which Jesus is the head. As Paul said, "whoever is in Christ is a new creation: the old things have passed away; behold, new things have come" (2 Cor. 5:17). In the Gospel of John, Jesus said, "What is born of flesh is flesh and what is born of the Spirit is spirit" (Jn. 3:6).

We often look to what someone does in an effort to define that person. This one is a teacher, a lawyer, a plumber, or an electrician. This is what people do, but this is not who they are. We do this to ourselves also. I am a father, a mother, a son, or a daughter. This describes a relationship that you have with someone; it is not who you are. Your nature as a Christian is a spiritual one. It is not defined by what you do or what role in a relationship you have. It is simply who you are. How you live comes from who you are, not what you do. Can you be a Christian in your job, whatever it is? Of course you can. Everyone needs to work at something to earn money to feed their families, to put a roof over their heads. Most people don't work in a Christian vocation, such as priest, pastor, or missionary. We are also not defined by our good works. Our good works come from who we are, not the other way around. It is the Holy Spirit in our hearts that will lead us to do good works. Being a Christian is not about doing this or not doing that; it is about following Jesus Christ, walking with Him, period.

"Think of what is above, not of what is on earth. For you have died, and your life is hidden with Christ in God" (Col. 3:2). All of you must die. Everything you think a Christian should or should not do, let it all die. Everything you use to define yourself, whether it be a job title, your relationships, or your good works, let it all die. It's too much work anyway trying to be someone or do something so we can look like we are "good" Christians. Meanwhile, our hearts are far from Him.

> For by grace you have been saved through faith, and this is not from you: it is the gift of God; it is not from works, so no one may boast. For we are His handiwork, created in Christ Jesus for the good works that God has prepared in advance, that we should live in them.
> (Ephesians 2:8)

Walking through life with Jesus is what being a Christian is about. The good works that we might do have already been prepared for us by God, "that we should live in them." As Christians, our lives are "hidden with Christ in God" so we don't have to try so hard; we just do. We do the good works that God has prepared for us.

Jesus did not have to try to do good works; He would see someone in need and fill the need. I don't think He set a goal each day for how many people He would heal, or how many demons He would cast out. He saw the multitudes and had compassion for them, so He fed them. He saw people that were hurting and needed to be healed, so He healed them. He saw people that needed to be reconciled with God and He forgave them their sins so that they could be, "the kindness of God would lead you to repentance" (Rom. 2:4). He observed the law perfectly but went beyond the letter of the law to the heart of it. He acted from His nature, not from what someone told Him He should do. In fact He went against what the religious leaders of His day said to do: He healed on the Sabbath, allowed His disciples to pick grain on the Sabbath, and His disciples didn't fast as the leaders did. He forgave sins when only God can forgive sins. All the things He did, the miracles, the healings, His teachings, all came from Him acting out of His nature and toward His purpose.

When we die to who we think we should be, who we think we are, how we think we should act, we open the door to let Jesus show us. I recommend that you open the door wide and let Him enter. He will show you who you are; a child of God, co-heir with Christ Jesus. He will show you how to act, because it will be Him acting through you. He will give you a life lived in the spirit: a life of abundance, a life of joy, and of peace. He will give you eternal life. Hallelujah! Praise be to our Lord Jesus Christ. Love Him with all your heart, with all your soul, and with all of your mind (Matt 12:30).

Healing Hearts

You know what I love about Jesus? Everything! I love that He gets to work on the heart of our problems. If you have a disagreement or argument with someone, you say, "Let's get to the heart of the problem." For most of us, the heart is the problem. "For from the fullness of the heart the mouth speaks. A good person brings forth good out of a store of goodness, but an evil person brings forth evil out of a store of evil" (Matt. 12:34). A few chapters later, Jesus says, "The things that come out of the mouth come from the heart, and they defile. For from the heart come evil thoughts, murder, adultery, unchastity, theft, false witness, blasphemy" (Matt. 15:18).

These are things that you see in the world every day. News channels run on a 24-hour cycle of these stories; magazines are written with nothing but these kinds of stories. It's easy to see how someone could grow to have a hardened and cynical heart with all being fed to them through these outlets and others. You are what you eat, my friends; not just what you put into your stomach, but also your mind and heart. This is why it is so important to spend time in God's word and in prayer and worship. Less time in the world, more time with the Lord. Not that we don't look at the issues of the world or care about them, but that we have them in perspective and see the world in the light of Christ.

I heard a radio pastor say something recently I liked. Reverend Wayne Monbleau from the "Let's talk about Jesus" radio service said something along the lines of, "Don't look at events with the eyes of the world and try to see God. Look at God, who is love, and with the eyes of God see the world." It's a completely different perspective. God loves us all. Instead of looking at events in the world and concluding that the world is crazy, or people are just no good, look at the world as God does, with compassion. See how many people suffer without a knowledge of Jesus. How many people need Jesus? All of us need Jesus.

I am fully convinced that the best thing I can do for this world, and for the people I love, is to live and preach the Gospel of Jesus Christ.

> So whether you eat or drink, or whatever you do, do everything for the glory of God. Avoid giving offense, whether to Jews or Greeks or the church of God, just as I try to please everyone in every way, not seeking my own benefit but that of the many, that they may be saved.
> (1 Corinthians 10:31)

When we allow the grace, mercy, and love of Jesus to work through us to the people in our lives, we give Jesus a chance to soften a hardened heart. It's a chance for Jesus to show them they are loved.

All of these conditions—malice, jealousy, anger, etc.—are all diseases of the heart. When these types of conditions are in your heart, your heart is diseased. You could say your heart is "dis"-eased, not at ease. As St. Augustine said in The confessions of St. Augustine, "My heart is restless, Lord, until it rests in you." Jesus works on your heart to heal everything and anything you allow Him to touch. Curing disease is one of His specialties, as the Bible is filled with stories of Jesus healing people. What we have to do is just bring our issues to Him, open our hearts, and allow Him to heal us. "Cast your worries upon Him for He cares for you" (1 Pet. 5:7). This is why spending time in the Scriptures and in prayer is so important; this is where we start to learn of Him and start to trust in Him. It's hard enough to really open up to someone you know, let alone someone that you don't know.

How does He do it? How does Jesus heal my heart? Good questions! Why don't you ask Him? I have never claimed to have all the answers, but I do know where to find them. In the Scriptures, Jesus healed different people in different ways: some with His touch, some with a word, some just touched His clothing. His ways of healing are specific to the one being healed; each one of us is different, and He gives each of us what we need when we need it. I believe that as we walk with Jesus, learning of Him in prayer and in the Scriptures, the Holy Spirit brings our issues to light in our hearts. Having a relationship with Jesus, we now can see them in the light of Christ and healing begins. When you receive the mercy, grace, and love of Jesus for yourself, and see that He really does care for you, the "dis"-ease melts away. It actually gets pushed out of the way by His mercy, grace, and love, because there won't be room in your heart for the other things. The cycle then starts for the continued healing of your heart. You start to trust Him and give Him more and more of yourself, and He continues to heal you.

Please don't think that all this happens in a day, a week, or a month. The Bible is not a book you rub three times and Jesus takes away all of your problems. No, my friends, I am not talking about any kind of quick fix for anything. The issues we deal with, the way we think, the diseases of our hearts took time to develop to what they are, and it will take time to heal them. This is why I speak of a daily walk with Jesus. This is the journey of a lifetime and it's your journey, not mine. I have my own walk with the Lord that has grown over the last ten years and continues to grow every day. One step at a time, one day at a time. "Do not worry about tomorrow; tomorrow will take care of itself. Sufficient for a day is its own evil" (Matt. 6:34). Once you taste and see the Lord is good, you will wonder how you ever lived without Him.

What we have to do is die; all of you must die. We must die to the diseases of our hearts and give them to Jesus; He will heal you. Can you imagine a life without any "dis"-ease in your heart? Jesus wants you to be free from all of them and He is the only one who can do it. "So if a Son frees you, then you will truly be free" (Jn. 8:36).

May God continue to bless you on your journey, as you daily grow in the grace and knowledge of our Lord Jesus Christ with a simplicity and purity of devotion to Him. Amen.

Who is He?

Who is Jesus Christ? The Bible gives Him many different names. In the book of Isaiah, He is called, "Wonderful Counselor, Mighty God, Eternal Father, Prince of Peace" (Isa. 9:6). Jesus calls Himself, "the good shepherd(Jn 10:11), the bread of life(Jn 6:35), the light of the world(John 8:12), the way, the truth and the life(Jn 14:6)." He is all of these things and much, much more. He is called many things by many people, but what is most important is this; who is Jesus to you? "Who do you say that I am?" (Matt. 16:15)

Ten years ago, Jesus was someone I claimed to believe in but didn't really know. I went to church because I was brought up that way. It's just what you do; you go to mass on Sunday. I heard the stories over and over again. The Bible never changed; Jesus never changed. I believed in Him as Lord and Savior, sang the songs, prayed the prayers, received communion, then left church and lived my life. I gave thought to Him mostly when I wanted something for myself and at Christmas and Easter. He had become another spoke on the wheel of my life, me at the center, and a spoke for family, friends, work, sports, entertainment, and then a spoke for Jesus. If this sounds like where you are in your relationship with Jesus, don't worry; there is hope.

One day I was praying and I realized I didn't know who I was talking to at that moment. I didn't know if I really believed someone was listening or that any good would come of my prayers; in fact, if any of this was real—God, Jesus, any of it. That's when I decided to honestly look into the truth of these things I had claimed to believe for my whole life. If it was all real, great, then I would start paying more attention and really learn more about my faith. If it wasn't real, well then, I would stop wasting my time and energy and just go on living my life as I saw fit. Can you guess which side of the coin I came down on? Jesus and God are real. Jesus is everything the Bible says He is and more.

Who Jesus is to me doesn't really help you though. Once again, what matters is who is Jesus to you? How much of a part of your life is He? When all is said and done, and you come before the Judgment Throne, will you hear, "Well done my good and faithful servant" (Matt. 25:21); or, what to me are the scariest words of scripture, "I never knew you. Depart from me, you evildoers" (Matt. 7:23)? I know which one I want to hear and which one I don't. I do not want Jesus to say to me, "Why do you call me, 'Lord, Lord,' but not do what I command?" (Lk. 6:46) The truth is that when we do listen to Him and do as He says, we are blessed. Our lives are made better; there is more joy in each day than ever before. So why don't we listen? We don't listen because we want to be the center hub on that wheel. We all must die to the idea that this life is about us. It is not; it is about Him. Paul says, "as a plan for the fullness of times, to sum up all things in Christ, in heaven and on earth" (Eph. 1:10). We must die to ourselves and put Jesus in the center of our wheel of life, with all spokes coming from and through Him out to the world. We must be Christ- centered, not self-centered.

"Blessed be the God and Father of our Lord Jesus Christ, who has blessed us in Christ with every spiritual blessing in the heavens" (Eph. 1:3). Notice the past tense of this verse, "who has blessed us." We have only to believe and to receive it for ourselves, then walk in this truth. There is nothing He would hold back from you. He has shown me these truths, and I know He will show you too. He treats us all the same. He loves us all and wants us to have a full knowledge of Him. Whatever you have done, whatever you have seen other people do in the name of Jesus, whatever you have been taught about Him, I pray that you can set it all aside and truly ask yourself, "Who is Jesus? Who is Jesus to me?" If the honest answer is, "I don't know," as it was for me, I pray that you will find out. I hope you will make it a priority to find the answers to all your questions. Jesus is not afraid of questions. He is, in fact, the one with the answers. The questions are about Him, so He has all the answers.

Come to Him with an open heart and an open mind, and let Him teach you about Himself. You can trust in Him. He will never lead you astray; He will only draw you closer to Himself. Once you get a glimpse of who He is and what He has done for you, a glimpse of the love that He has for you, there can be only one response. I love you Jesus with all of my heart, with all my mind, with all my soul, and with all my strength. Then you will start to grow in the grace and knowledge of Jesus with a simplicity and purity of devotion to Him.

BE LOVED

There is a word used in the New Testament often that I like—it is "beloved." We are the beloved children of God. The degree of our awareness of this, I think, has a direct correlation to our own self-image. If we are truly beloved children, and we know this, is it possible to have a poor or negative self-image? I would like to take this word and combine it with a verse from Psalms. Psalm 46 verse 10 says, "Be still, and know that I am God." I'm sure all of you have heard these words of scripture. I would like to add to this as a meditation for us all: Be still, and Be Loved, and know that I am God.

The love that God has for each of us is beyond measure, for we are all priceless in His sight. I believe the closest we can come to knowing this kind of love is the love of a parent for his/her child. How many people would say that they would give their lives for their spouses, or their children? I think most of us would say that, but very few ever have the chance to prove it. (Thank God for that!) What has God done? God proved His love for us. God loves us all so much that He gave His only begotten son to die on the cross. Jesus said, "I came so that they might have life and have it more abundantly" (Jn. 10:10). He died on the cross for us, for all of us, so that we would have life. "No one has greater love than this, to lay down one's life for one's friends" (Jn. 15:13).

Think of this in your meditation: Be still, and Be Loved, and know that I am God. Jesus loves you; He gave His life for you so that you might have life in Him. "I am the vine, you are the branches. Whoever remains in me and I in him will bear much fruit, because without me you can do nothing" (Jn. 15:5). He not only died for us, He lived for us. His whole purpose in coming was to save us, to reconcile us with God, and to show us how much we are loved. He died to show us God's mercy toward us, His unending grace in which we stand. Right now, this very moment, you are standing in the grace of God. Your sins have been washed away by the blood of the Lamb. Jesus has put His robe of righteousness on you, so that you could appear before the Father as He does: spotless, without mark or defect, without blemish. This is how God sees us, all of us, who have received Jesus Christ as our Lord and Savior, been born again, and filled with the Holy Spirit. What an amazing love this is, beyond measure, beyond our comprehension.

What about all my faults? Covered. What about my past sins? Washed away. "There is no condemnation for those who are in Christ Jesus" (Rom. 8:1). Here and now, in this meditation, simply focus on how much Jesus loves you and let yourself BE LOVED.

(pause)

If we are loved this much, how can we have a poor or negative self-image? We all must die to whatever else we base our self-image on and let it be based on the love God has for us. I'll say it again; you are priceless in the sight of God. You are loved. There is no greater feeling than that of being loved. Love can crack open the hardest of hearts; love can bring tears of joy. The love of Jesus can bring the strongest of men to their knees, can cause a heart to repent, to forgive, to change. The love of Jesus, if received as it's given, freely, leaves us all with no choice but to love each other.

If I am loved so wonderfully, so completely, with all of my flaws, sins, and imperfections, how can I not love those that are just like me? Jesus does. The love Jesus has for me cannot be held in this body, in this broken vessel, in this human heart: it must be shared. I write these things that I might share His love with you; that you would receive it in your heart; that you would be encouraged to grow in the grace and knowledge of Jesus Christ with a simplicity and purity of devotion to Him; that through my sharing, you would be built up in your most holy faith and come to know His love for you; and that you would share His love as well.

Mark 10:42-45

PERFECT?

I would like to share with you a little secret of mine. Don't tell anyone but I am not perfect. There, I said it; I am not perfect. Whew! It feels good to get that off my chest. Ask my wife and my son; they'll tell you I am far from perfect. Guess what, my friends? You are not perfect either. I'm sorry to be the one to tell you, but it's true. None of us are perfect.

Here's another little secret about me. I don't even try to be perfect. A lot of people wake up each day and try to be perfect in everything they do, trying very hard not to make any mistakes, even harder to hide their flaws and missteps; some to the point of denying that they have any flaws or ever make a mistake. They are always right in everything that they do and if you disagree with them, you are obviously the one that is wrong. I think we all know someone like this. I do not try to be perfect because it is not possible, I am a human being. I make mistakes, a lot of them. I have many flaws and imperfections in myself, but I don't try to hide them or deny they exist. That would be too exhausting; it would take up too much of my time and energy if I did. What I do each morning is wake up and thank God for a new day. Then I "strive to know the Lord" (Hos. 6:3). He is perfect.

The degree that I allow Jesus to live through me is the degree of my perfection, but it's not mine; it's His. If it's Him living through us, then everything we do we will do to the best of our abilities. Jesus is alive in us and works in us, and through us in every area of our lives if we let Him. I have a wife, a son, a job, and many people that I care about in my life. Of course I want to be a good husband and father, I want to do a good job for my customers, and I hope each day is to be better in all areas of my life. I have found the best way to accomplish all of this is to, every day, learn more about Jesus. "Draw near to God and He will draw near to you" (James 4:8). I continue on in prayer, in worship, and in the reading of the Scriptures. "Your word is a lamp for my feet, a light for my path" (Ps. 119:105). I have found this verse to be true time and time again over the last ten years.

He helps me every day to be a good husband, a good father, to do a good job at work, all because He leads me and guides me onto right paths. He knows which way I should go, and I trust Him because He has shown Himself to be a faithful friend.

Jesus helps us in all areas of life each and every day—obviously in our spiritual lives but also in our daily, practical lives. He helps us especially in one of the hardest parts of life, dealing with other people. He helps us to deal with people with love and kindness, compassion and mercy. He gives us wisdom and knowledge to know what to say and when to say it, to know what to do and when to do it. He helps us to see that none of us are perfect. This is not to put any of us down, but so that we might have compassion for all the other imperfect people in the world. If you could have every interaction with people, be it pleasant, nice, even joyful, wouldn't that help to improve your day? Wouldn't that help you to have a better, more positive attitude throughout the day? Wouldn't it make you better at whatever you were trying to do- better husband, better father, better at work? As we allow Him to live in us and through us, He changes our hearts and our minds so that we would be "conformed to the image of His Son" (Rom. 8:29). As John the Baptist said, "He must increase; I must decrease" (Jn. 3:30).

What about the people that aren't pleasant or nice? Having the light of Christ in us, we can greet them with understanding and compassion. We shouldn't let them bring us down or change our attitudes. We should show them the love of Christ that dwells in us by how we live our lives and hopefully lift them up. If they respond favorably, we have won over our brother; if not, hopefully we have softened their hearts just a little bit. Every time they encounter someone who lets the light of Christ shine through; it is a chance that their hearts might be softened even more. Remember our job as Christians is not to save anyone, because Jesus does that. Our job is simply to lift Him up and He will draw all men to Himself. God is working on each of us to draw us to Himself, and in His time it will be done. May we be open to Him so that He might use us to draw those that have drifted away back into the fold.

Whether or not we are perfect does not draw people to Jesus Christ. Trying to be perfect does not help us in living happy, joyful lives. What draws people to Jesus is a heart of love and kindness, a caring and compassionate heart, a heart of mercy and forgiveness. These qualities of the heart do help us to live happy, joyful lives and draw people to Jesus Christ. Having Jesus living in us and working through us is a win-win for us and for everyone that we meet. We all must die to our idea of being perfect and what perfection looks like, to let Jesus lead us into His perfection.

John
7: 37-38

Turn Around

You know what I love about Jesus? Everything. I love the fact that He never gives up on us. He has His hand stretched toward each of us every day. He is truly a faithful friend, even when we are faithless. I said earlier that I have always believed in Him, but that in the past He didn't have much impact on my daily life. I knew He was there, but I continued to walk in my own path, my own direction; never turning around to look at Him; never letting Him in any more than I was comfortable with. I had my back to Him for a long time, but He never gave up on me.

My friends, He will never give up on you either. His desire is that all of us come to a knowledge of God. God's desire is for no one to perish but have eternal life with Him. I turned around in my faith almost ten years ago and have been walking with Jesus ever since. Now I can echo the apostle Peter's words, "Master, to whom shall we go? You have the words of eternal life" (Jn. 6:68). Every day we are alive is a chance to turn to Him and learn of Him. Every day we are alive is a day we can show Him to someone that doesn't know Him, expressing in our actions and words His love, His mercy, and His forgiveness; that through us, they might see Him.

Jesus has many ways to call someone to Himself, to get them to turn around. I believe He can and will use anything or anyone to draw people to Himself, but they first must be open to Him. I pray that this book will open your heart to Him; that you would be encouraged to know Him more, to grow deeper in love with Him. My brothers and sisters, Jesus is always here for us. "And behold, I am with you always, until the end of the age" (Matt. 28:20). If you are in trouble, turn to Jesus. If you are in hard times, turn to Jesus. If you are joyful, turn to Jesus. He will weep with you when you weep and rejoice with you when you rejoice. Turn to Him; He will always be there for you. He will never stop trying to reach you; He will never give up on you. He loves you. He loves you so much that He gave His life for you; that you would have life, and have it more abundantly.

Sometimes we get so focused on ourselves we don't think we have time for Jesus. We have so much to do each day that we barely take the time to breathe. Thank God breathing is involuntary or some of us would forget to do it. Many of us are so busy chasing our goals and dreams, taking care of our families, trying to make a life that we're not really living. Many of us never enjoy the day we've been given because we are always looking to a better day—a day when all of our hopes and dreams do come true; a day when we will finally get to relax and enjoy life. Each day is a gift, and if you're not careful, this day could slip away from you just like many other days in your life. Too busy "living" to have a life doesn't look like much of a life at all; always waiting for something to change, keep on keeping on when there is no joy in it at all. Everyone else is doing it so I guess this is just how it is. This, my friends, is not how it should be, not how it can be; this is not what a life with Jesus is like at all.

Jesus said, "Without me you can do nothing" (Jn. 15:5). In Him we have abundant life—a life worth living. Our hopes and dreams are important, taking care of our families is important and Jesus knows this. "I can do all things through Christ who strengthens me" (Phil. 4:13, NKJV). He wants to show you how. He wants you to have the best life possible, but first you must turn to Him. We all must die to our own vision of our lives and learn to see the life that Jesus has for us. A life better than you thought possible; a life with a purpose greater than ourselves; a life filled with joy, peace, and love in the Holy Spirit.

    I pray for all of you, my friends, that you would turn around, take Him by the hand, and walk with Him all of your days. You will see that everything I have shared with you about Him is true and someday when someone asks you what you love about Jesus, you will not hesitate to say, "Everything!!!"

Pick Up Your Cross

"Whoever wishes to come after me must deny himself, take up his cross, and follow me. For whoever wishes to save his life will lose it, but whoever loses his life for my sake will find it" (Matt. 16:24). All four gospels have Jesus saying these same words with little variation. He might have different words leading up to and coming after this verse, but they all have this verse of scripture in their gospel accounts. That tells me something of its importance to Jesus and to the gospel writers. It was important enough to put into their gospel accounts, knowing that the other writers had already covered this teaching. Matthew, Mark, Luke, and John all wanted us to know this truth.

This is the scripture that inspired the title of this book, "All of you must die." I don't mean a literal, heart-stopping death and neither does Jesus. All of us, myself included, must die to everything and anything that would get between us and Jesus. "Whoever loves father or mother more than me is not worthy of me, and whoever loves son or daughter more than me is not worthy of me; and whoever does not take up his cross and follow after me is not worthy of me" (Matt. 10:37). Salvation is a free gift of God's grace in Jesus Christ, but that doesn't mean it won't cost you anything. It will cost you everything. It will cost you your life. Better yet, it will cost you what you perceive as your life. "Amen, amen, I say to you, unless you eat the flesh of the Son of Man and drink His blood, you do not have life within you" (Jn. 6:53). If Jesus is not within you, then what kind of life do you have?

"Now those who belong to Christ Jesus have crucified their flesh with its passions and desires. If we live in the Spirit, let us also follow the Spirit" (Gal. 5:24). Your life is in the Spirit. Everything we associate with our lives in the world—our jobs, whether we are male or female, husbands, wives, black or white, rich or poor—has nothing to do with our true lives in the Spirit. This is the ultimate meaning of denying yourself, picking up your cross, and following Jesus. This is what "All of you" must die means. Everything that you identify with as being "you" must be released. It must die so you can grow in a life of the Spirit.

This is what will help you to see that we are all the same; we are all of the same Spirit. We are the spiritual Body of Christ here on earth. This, I believe, is the key to us "being one" as Jesus prayed in John chapter 17:

> I pray not only for them, but also for those who will believe in me through their word, so that they may all be one, as you, Father, are in me and I in you, that they also may be in us, that the world may believe that you sent me.
> (John 17:20)

I ask you, is there any greater purpose for the Body of Christ than this? That we would be one and that the world would know God sent His son not to condemn the world, but that through Him they might be saved?

How are we going to be as one if we only see ourselves through the lens of the world, which constantly divides us? We must see each other through the eyes of the Spirit and help and encourage one another in Jesus Christ. The journey we are on, the ability to let go of ourselves, to die to ourselves, is not an easy one. Jesus knows this and is here for each of us every day to guide us in His word, to help us see with the eyes of the Spirit. "The Advocate, the holy Spirit that the Father will send in my name—he will teach you everything and remind you of all that I told you" (Jn. 14:26). He will teach us all things about Jesus—who we are in Him and who He is in us. He will help us to die to ourselves; He will help us to pick up our crosses because He has done it Himself. We are not alone on this journey or in this life; we are never alone.

The journey of dying to ourselves and allowing Jesus to live through us is a lifelong journey; an adventure like you've never been on before. All the "how tos" and "what to dos" will become clearer and easier to see and understand, as you consistently walk with Jesus every day. I sincerely hope, my friends, that you will join me in this daily prayer:

Heavenly Father, I pray on this day and every day that I would grow in the grace and knowledge of Jesus Christ, with a simplicity and purity of devotion to Him.

LAST CHAPTER

In this last chapter, my friends, I would just like to share with you that these words do not come from someone who doesn't live in the "real world." My walk with the Lord is what keeps me going, He sustains me in all of life's many trials.

Since 2011 or so, my wife started to show symptoms of what we now know to be several rare diseases. She has not been able to work since July 2013. Her health kept getting worse, new symptoms came and doctors could not figure out what was going on. She was diagnosed with Common Variable Immune Deficiency, basically having no immune system, and Fibromyalgia. It wasn't until seeing our fifth neurologist in 2015 that we received her diagnosis of Hereditary Spastic Paraplegia and Primary Lateral Sclerosis. Both are rare and both have no known cure. Both are progressive.

She has had the pain and suffering of all these conditions, and I have been able to do nothing but watch her get worse and worse. I cannot relieve her of any pain; I cannot make any of this go away. She is the love of my life, the most beautiful person inside and out that I have ever met. She has handled all of this with a grace that is unbelievable and a faith in Jesus Christ that has only grown stronger. As for me, Jesus has been my strength in all of this. He has been with us each and every step, as we walk through the valley of the shadow of death. It has been just that, walking in the valley of the shadow of death since 2013. Death has come very close a few times, but the Lord has brought her through.

I heard a saying that life is not about waiting for the storm to pass, it is about learning to dance in the rain. This is what Jesus has done for us, like Shadrach, Meshach, and Abednego in the book of Daniel. The furnace has been turned up seven times and the Lord has been with us dancing in the flames. He is the reason that we can still laugh, smile, and enjoy the life we have. He has brought us closer together through it all.

I do believe everything happens for a reason. I don't know why this is happening to us, but I trust in God that He will work it all out for good. Before my wife's health issues started, my sister was diagnosed with ALS in 2010. I went to the Lord in prayer asking why. She has four kids, she's so young, she has so much more to live for. I heard the Lord ask me, "Do you trust Me with your life?" I said, "Why are You even asking me this? You know that I do." He said, "Trust me with hers." It was very clear, unmistakable. I am to trust Him with my life; I am to trust Him with the life of everyone that I love.

So my testimony of Jesus Christ does not come from a book; it does not come from what someone else has said or told me. My testimony of Jesus comes from His active, daily participation in my life. I wouldn't trade my walk with the Lord for anything in the world. It just keeps getting better. He keeps showing me new things, teaching me more of who He is and who I am in Him every day. He is my Lord, my Savior, the King of Kings, the Lord of Lords, my Prince of Peace, my wonderful counselor, my best friend. He has never left me; He has never forsaken me; He gave His life for me. How could I do any less?

What He has done for me, He wants to do for you. He loves us all and He wants you to know that love in real time, in your real circumstances, every day of your life. All you

ALL OF YOU MUST DIE ! (SPIRITUALLY SPEAKING)

have to do is die. Then grow in the grace and knowledge of our Lord Jesus Christ, with a simplicity and purity of devotion to Him.

May God bless you all on your journey.

www.ingramcontent.com/pod-product-compliance
Ingram Content Group UK Ltd.
Pitfield, Milton Keynes, MK11 3LW, UK
UKHW042004230426
12048UKWH00009B/543